LET'S GET PUBLICITY

AND GET IT RIGHT

A Guide to Publicity and Public Relations for Voluntary Organisations

By

David P. Saint

Cover Design and Illustrations

By Ron Branagan

© Printforce Limited

British Library Cataloguing in Publication
Data
Saint, David, 1952-
Let's Get Publicity and get it right.
1. Voluntary organisations. Public relations
I. Title
659.2'88
ISBN 0-948834-21-8

CONTENTS

CONTENTS

Introduction

This book is essentially about two subjects - image and information. Both are closely interlinked, and both are of vital importance to every voluntary organisation.

Our "Image" is the public face of our organisation. The image we project will have a fundamental effect upon the way people think of us, and react to us. This includes potential members, their relatives, potential helpers, leaders, committee members, supporters, sponsors and contributors. It includes people you may want to help, or from whom you may want help. It is therefore vital that you are sure that your 'image' (which we shall define shortly) gets across the **right** messages about your organisation (and we shall be considering what they might be, as well.) Image is in some ways a passive, but no less important form of communication.

'Information' may therefore be described as active communication. Information consists of specific facts which your public or publics (another term we shall later define) should know. It needs to be presented clearly, attractively, and in the correct order.

This distinction perhaps also helps us to distinguish between public relations and publicity. There are some areas of overlap, but essentially public relations involves, as its name implies, the building of a relationship with your public. Publicity is the planned communication of information to that public.

'Image' and 'information' messages are very important to each other. To illustrate this, let us consider the following example announcements. Your favourite television programme is interrupted for a News Flash. The newscaster appears with his tie undone, soup stains on his shirt, his hair wet and uncombed since his shower, and makes the following announcement in a bored and slurred voice.

"The Government has just announced emergency measures to cope with a power shortage following the temporary closure of half the country's power stations for emergency safety inspections. All consumers are asked to cut back on their use of electricity by 25% forthwith to avoid widespread power cuts."

How much attention do you pay to this announcement?

Alternatively, your same evening's viewing may be interrupted by an impeccably dressed newscaster, who fixes the camera with an urgent stare, and makes the following announcement:

"Somebody seems to think we may be a bit short of electricity this week - something to do with reservoirs being empty, or problems at power stations - something like that, anyway. So we are all asked to do our bit and turn off a few lights and things."

How much attention do you pay to **this** announcement?

Clearly, the image presented and the information conveyed both contribute to the effect upon the audience.

Within this book you will find ideas and advice on ways of presenting a positive image to people inside and outside your organisation, and on ways of presenting information to those people. The task requires a degree of discipline, and a lot of sustained effort if the true benefits are to be reaped.

If possible, the organisation should have one person to shoulder the responsibility for publicity and public relations, and to develop some of the skills required. This person should not become cut off in an esoteric world of press releases and posters. He or she will need to be closely involved with all that the organisation does, to be able to communicate this to the outside world and, where necessary, to affect the way the organisation presents itself and its activities.

It is possible to exist as an organisation without taking any positive steps towards publicity and public relations. It is likely that, by neglecting to do so, the organisation will miss out on innumerable opportunities to further its cause, increase its membership, or obtain financial and practical support. We hope that this book will help you to maximise these opportunities.

Summary

Publicity and Public Relations is about the communication of *image* and *information*.

This is a large responsibility. Try to appoint one person to be responsible for co-ordinating all this type of activity for your organisation.

Actually, Madam Reporter . . .
. . . I'm the Club Treasurer — This gentleman is our Publicity Officer!

First Principles

What are we to communicate

a) The image of our organisation.

What do we mean by this? Start by writing down some adjectives which you hope an outsider would apply to your organisation. Here are some to choose from: caring; efficient; lively; fun; cost-conscious; dynamic; responsible; authoritative; relevant; interesting. There may be others you would add to the list. Now consider these adjectives against the 'public faces' of your organisation. These may include your meeting place, mini-bus, logo, headed paper, literature, the way your members present themselves (particularly if yours is a uniformed organisation), and what your members say about the organisation.

These may have little effect on public opinion individually, but put together they build up into an overall picture which may not be the one you want. To take a specific example, if your minibus is unwashed and rusty, will you be seen as cost conscious, not spending money on car washes and paint jobs, or will you be seen as careless with resources, not properly maintaining expensive assets?

Some of the messages you wish to communicate may be contradictory. Perhaps you wish your organisation to be seen as responsible **and** fun. It may well be both, of course, but it may be difficult to convey both of these elements on, say, your headed notepaper. In this case you will need to decide which is more important, and concentrate on that, perhaps hinting at the other element, as long as it does not detract from the key message.

Once you have gone through this process of describing your organisation in a few select words (a good job for a committee!), it will be a lot easier to ensure that every time a member of the public notices anything about your organisation it reinforces what you want them to think about you.

b) Information.

The information you wish to communicate may be basic facts, such as when and where you meet, and what you do. It may be specific information about an event you are staging, that you wish people to attend. It may be that you will want to communicate opinion, or try to affect people's attitudes about certain matters.

As with your image, it is vital to be absolutely clear about what information you wish to communicate. Remember that we are subjected to a torrent of information every day, and that the public may not be as keenly interested in your organisation as you are. It is therefore necessary to select the key messages only, and to communicate these in an appealing way. Far better to select the information which must be conveyed, and restrict yourself to that. If for example, you plan a jumble sale to raise funds for your campaign about homelessness, the posters, leaflets etc., should focus on the details of the sale. If you want to influence opinion, wait until the punters have arrived at the sale, then give them more detailed information about your campaign.

Having prepared your information with this in mind, go back over it to ensure that you have not left any important questions unanswered. For example, if your organisation has an obscure title that is not immediately self-explanatory it may be a help to add a sentence in brackets after it, to explain its significance to the uninitiated. If the information concerns a fund-raising event is there a reference to what the money is for? If it concerns a form of entertainment, does the title adequately describe the content and style of the performance, or is a little extra explanation necessary?

Why do we wish to communicate this information?

This may seem a ridiculous question, but if we answer it it will help us to write and design the document in such a way that it more precisely achieves our objectives.

It may be that our prime objective is to obtain money, or support, or attendance at an event. Perhaps we want to please the people we are writing about, or to interest possible new members. If we are quite clear about our purpose, it will be easier to start to compose the text of the communication, and to make sure that it concentrates on the matter in hand, without including all sorts of red herrings which will simply confuse the reader.

To whom do we wish to communicate?

This is an important question, as it will govern how we write and present the information, and by what means it is circulated. It may be nice to communicate to the whole world, but what is our appropriate public, or publics? This may change for different pieces of information in different ways, and different places. For example, we may only wish to communicate to our own members. It this is the case an internal newsletter is far more appropriate than a letter in the local paper. We may want to attract people to a fund raising Bingo session, in which case the newspaper probably would be a more appropriate medium to use. Whatever your information, it should be possible to classify your **ideal** target audience by age, sex, interest, location or occupation. The more precisely you can do this, the better. Then, as you write the information, conjure up a picture in your mind of a typical example of that type of person, and write specifically for him or her, addressing their needs and interests. When considering the design and style of presentation of the information, picture your typical example again.

Finally, when you plan where to place the information, consider the places your typical example is most likely to find it. On a church noticeboard? In the pub? On the sports page of the local paper? Beside the Births, Marriages and Deaths announcements? Consider your target market at all stages of the production of publicity and public relations material; then you only have to get the timing right, and you can do no more!

How much should we spend?

This is an important question, as some publicity activity can be very expensive. Editorials in newspapers, posters in shops, announcements at meetings etc., are usually free, but you have less control over what is said, and when or even if it is said. Sometimes you will wish to take no chances, and buy some form of publicity to guarantee the information being placed. You may well decide to spend money on the production of literature, posters, button badges, car stickers, etc. But how much?

The key to answering this question is to ask three others. First, what is the publicity intended to achieve? Second, what is the value of that achievement to us? Third, how likely are we to be successful?

The publicity may be intended to achieve something very measureable, such as attendance at an event. Is it worth spending 5p for every person encouraged to attend? Or 50p? Or £1.00? Perhaps the achievement is measureable, but not in such simple terms. Perhaps you wish to attract new members. You will have to decided on a notional figure that you are prepared to spend. Perhaps you simply want to produce button badges and car stickers to make existing members feel a greater sense of 'belonging'.

When we are clear about the objective, and we have decided on its value to us (and therefore how much we are prepared to spend) we can consider this in relation to what we plan to do. It may be that our plans will have to be cut down to size to fit the budget.

It is always worth considering the equivalent cost effectiveness of our plans at this point. Are we using our resources in the way that most precisely addresses the target audience, in the way they will be most likely to notice? An advertisement in a rural newspaper, for example, may be more expensive than writing a letter to every householder in the village where you are trying to start a local group. The letter would certainly be read by more people, and you would have the opportunity to include more information, separate leaflets, etc.

In considering the costs, remember to include all the elements, including (to return to the example in the last paragraph) those extra leaflets, the envelopes, the stamps (unless they are to be delivered by volunteers), and so on.

Overall presentation

To underpin our publicity activity we would do well to develop a strong corporate identity. Major companies spend huge sums of money to try to ensure that when we see a shell we think of a petrol company; when we see a black horse we think of a bank.

It is possible, without spending hundreds of thousands of pounds, to move towards the benefits of a strong corporate identity, particularly on a local scale.

What are the elements of this corporate identity?

1) The name of your organisation.

It may be too well established to change it (which is a good thing - if it means something to the general public, and not just to your members). But take a hard look at it, and consider whether it is sufficiently concise, punchy and explanatory.

2) The Logo.

This is the symbol associated with your organisation (such as the shell and black horse already mentioned earlier). If your organisation is part of a large body with its own logo there will probably be quite strict rules governing its use - you should find out what these are. If you have no logo it is worth considering developing one. The symbol can be created from the initials of your organisation, something associated with the place in which you meet, or something which suggests the type of organisation you are.

3) Strap Line.

It is sometimes unavoidable that the name of an organisation is not a good description of it. Sometimes a short phrase or sentence added to the name, used on publicity material etc., can get across an additional message—"Midland Bank, the Listening Bank" for example.

4) House Colour.

(The term 'house' is a common jargon term worth getting used to - it simple means the organisation in question). Later in the book we will be discussing the use of colour to brighten up designs, but more fundamental is the use of colour on your name, logo and strap line. Again, you may be constrained by the house colour of the larger organisation of which you are a part, so do check. If not, these are some of the factors you should consider. The house colour should be associated with all your publicity material other than those simply printed black on white, so it should be versatile. It should be a standard colour which printers can obtain easily and not have to mix. It is a good idea to specify a particular colour by Pantone number. This is a generally recognised way of identifying particular shades of colour, so that you can ensure that you always use **exactly** the colour you intend. A printer should be able to show you a Pantone 'swatch' of colours so that you can pick out the one you want. You should keep a careful note of the number and letter on it. Thereafter you will only have to give this reference to any printer, and you will always get the same shade.

5) House Style.

This is the particular way in which you present things. Unless you expect to produce a lot of printed material it would be too pedantic to have too many rules, but a few general guidelines will help your documents relate to each other, and look part of an organised package. You may, for example, always choose to use the same typeface. Perhaps text will be laid out in a standard way—either indenting new paragraphs, or leaving a line between each, for example. The overall objective is to produce documents which 'hang together' and reinforce the overall corporate identity which you are trying to establish.

It may also be that there are specific messages which you wish to continually reinforce, in much the same way as your strap line. It can help to use the same form of words each time, so that the message becomes memorable simply because it is repeated — just like television advertising.

When we have established all these elements of our corporate identity, we should plan to make every possible use of them. General stationery items such as letterheads and compliment slips are obvious opportunities, but so is every other piece of paper you have printed—newsletters, leaflets, posters, and so on. Many organisations produce other items to reinforce their corporate identity, and members are often keen to have them. These include button badges, T shirts, car stickers, key fobs— you name it. Because they are popular with members they can often be sold to them, which helps to cover the initial cost.

It is a useful and interesting exercise to think through just how many ways you can reinforce your corporate identity and its associated messages. On the minibus? Meeting place? Brief case? Look at what commercial companies do to keep themselves in the forefront of your mind. What can you learn from them— and apply at a fraction of the cost?

Evaluation

Once you have done all you can to communicate your image, and your information, it is tempting to think that you have finished. You have not! It is most important that you try to review how successful was each piece of publicity, and which worked but proved to be too expensive to be justified. It is only with this information that you will be able to be more successful next time.

There are a number of ways of doing this. The most effective is to ask every person who responds to your messages which ones they saw, and what was it about them that worked. For example, one of your members might go along the queue outside your jumble sale and ask each of the people queuing how they heard of it. Did somebody tell them? Did they see your advert in the paper? The poster? (If so, where was the one they saw?) or the handbill? The answers will give you some clue as to which method attracted the most people, and which did not.

Summary

Be clear about what is to be communicated.

- image (what is appropriate)
- information (what are the key messages?)

Be clear about the reasons for communicating your image, and the information.

Be precise about who the information is aimed at.

Consider the cost implications.

Develop a strong Corporate Identity to underpin all your communications activity.

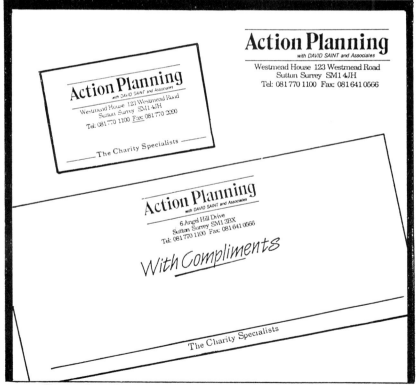

Examples of corporate stationery showing a Letterhead, Compliment Slip and Business Card

Internal Public Relations

In this and the following chapter we continue to draw a distinction between publicity and Public Relations. Here we are concerned with the general 'personality' of our organisation—is it one that people feel drawn to? In the next chapter we shall consider the circulation of information within the organisation.

Before we set out to invest time and money on trying to get our organisation noticed, we should ensure that, in every respect, it is worth noticing. When planning publicity and public relations we should, therefore, start at the very heart of the organisation. We should ensure that the members feel good about the body they belong to, and that they will project a good image of it.

This will require some considerable thought about the nature of the organisation and what it should be. It is perhaps worth going back to the list of adjectives we prepared to describe the organisation in the last chapter, and to consider how much like those idealised statements it really is. Would the present members use those adjectives to describe the activities, leadership and general style of operation to which they have become accustomed? The best way to find out is to ask them.

You may do this in a semi-formal way, which can be fun for all that. A questionnaire can be prepared in which each member is asked to note down his or her views on a number of topics, either by ticking an attribute such as excellent, good, fair, poor, appalling. Space may be left for other comments or suggestions. The topics will vary from one organisation to another, but you might pick out a few of your own. The question about each might be phrased thus "How effective is .... in giving the public a good impression of our organisation?" Or thus "Please indicate which of the following have a good or bad effect on the way you might feel about our organisation". Topics might include the programme of activities, the leadership, amount of consultation of members, uniform, discipline, formalities, costs, the meeting place, level of communication, or design of materials (such as badges, headed paper, etc.).

This exercise may be a salutary lesson in the way the members perceive the leadership, and might give some useful ideas on improving things as a spin-off. However, the main objective should be to obtain the views of existing members about ways of making the organisation more attractive and relevant to outsiders. To do the job properly, of course, it would be best to seek the views of outsiders as well, in a separate but parallel questionnaire, and then to compare the two sets of answers.

If you are not prepared to take the risk of finding out what people **really** think about you, or if there are other reasons which make the exercise too complicated, you should still carry it out in part, by asking the views of a few select people who you can trust for an honest answer. If there is no alternative but to do it yourself, you will have to think very carefully and honestly about each question.

Having completed the exercise you should have a reasonably clear idea of the way the organisation is viewed from the inside. It is likely that this will, in part, be reflected in the view held by outsiders—assuming they have noticed you yet. If you are unhappy about that view, or parts of it, you may be pleased if outsiders have **not** noticed you yet! The next stage, clearly, is to set those parts of your house in order that would contribute to a negative view of it from outside. How you do that is beyond the scope of this book, but in general terms it is likely to call for the improving of standards and attitudes. Only when this review and subsequent 'spring clean' has been completed should you seriously consider exposing your organisation to outside attention. If we cannot project a positive image to people inside the organisation, we can hardly expect to be successful in communicating it to people outside.

If the lessons learned from these exercises are applied, it is likely that the members will have increased pride in belonging, will feel good about the organisation, and will therefore communicate enthusiastically about it to outsiders. They become eager ambassadors, and thus your most valuable public relations arm.

Summary

Identify the feelings of members about the organisation.

Improve areas shown to require attention.

Aim to develop members' pride in the organisation to which they belong.

Fiery Cross

Each letter represents a different person. Each person has only to contact 3 or 4 others. The result is that 12 people get the message from A. Each of the people at the end of the chain could have their own list to contact if more people are involved. Each person should have a copy of the chart.

When a message has to go round, the leader only has to contact the leaders of each cell, who in turn have to contact the small number of people in that cell with the message. Thus each person has a maximum of 6 contacts to make. If the message is important you may wish to included a checking mechanism, by which people are asked to report back to the cell leader, or overall leader, when they have received the message. It is likely that this system will make use of the telephone.

A word about the use of this instrument if you wish to be really effective. You doubtless already try to make most of your calls at 'off peak' times, but that can often take you straight into many people's mealtimes or, worse still, the soap opera hour. Although you cannot possibly make allowances for all eventualities, by some careful selection of phoning time you can ensure that most of your calls will receive a reasonably warm and attentive welcome!

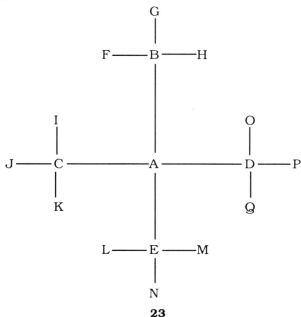

Have a pad beside you, not only to remind you of what you want to say to people, but also to make a note of any key points that they say to you, which you may wish to remember.

As we suggested earlier, word of mouth is an effective way of relating past events, and it can be valuable to ask members to recount recent experiences for the benefit of all. Not only does this help that member increase his or her confidence in 'public speaking', and give them a moment of stardom, it also reinforces the value of such activities to other members who perhaps choose not to attend.

There is something to be said for having a regular slot in meetings for such reporting back. Children particularly welcome an opportunity to share their new experiences with a wider audience, and it might be interesting to give the members this opportunity, perhaps once a month. Anybody can stand up and give their 'news'. You will have laid down guidelines as to whether or not this should relate exclusively to their experiences in connection with the organisation, or whether it could include family news, etc. Initially it may be necessary to 'encourage' one or two people to break the ice, but once the practice is established there should be no shortage of volunteers.

Whenever the spoken word is used for communicating information, especially if it is important, consideration should be given to finding some way of backing this up with a written reminder. This is not always possible, of course, but when it is, it can be a great help.

24

Notes Home

Whether you are preparing notes for children to take home to their parents, or *aide-mémoire* for adults to take away with them, there are a number of key points to remember to ensure that they fulfil their objective.

First, you should recognise that some may not reach their destination, and you should therefore plan some back-up reminder system if possible.

Second, you should make it clear when handing them out, and on the notes themselves, who they are for, and what they are about. Are they to be handed on to parents? Is the subject matter urgent, or even interesting? Do the messages apply to every member, or only those over a certain age, or participating in a specific activity?

Attention should be paid to clarity of layout and reproduction. It does not take much extra time or money to ensure that the note is legible, easy to read by virtue of being broken up into short paragraphs, and clear about its content through headings and sub-headings. Remember that this is just a note, so keep it brief.

If a response is required, make this very clear. Have a response slip, either at the foot of the note to be cut off, or as a separate sheet stapled to the note. Make it clear when the slip has to be returned by, and to whom. Ensure that by returning the slip the reader is not left without vital information which only appears on it, and nowhere else.

Noticeboards

Noticeboards are an opportunity for spreading information. This opportunity is often wasted. All too often they are untidy, unattractive, uncared for and unread. Properly used they can become a lively forum for the exchange of information and the latest news. Here's how!

The position of the noticeboard is important. It must be in a location which is frequently visited by all members, and where they can stop to read it in comfort, without causing an obstruction. It should be at such a height that all members can read all parts of it.

The noticeboard itself should be attractive but nondescript—it is the messages on it that need to stand out and be noticed. However, the appearance of the board and the way the notices can be organised can be enhanced with a few simple additions. In many ways it can be used like the front page of a newspaper. It should have a heading—something a little less obvious and more appealing than 'Notices'! If you have different types of notices, the board can be divided up with coloured ribbon pinned in place. This might mark out sections for different ages, or the Sports Sections, or News. Each of these separate sections should have its own heading in bright, attractive lettering.

The information on the noticeboard should be changed regularly, so that members know that they have to look at it frequently to keep up to date. There should be other incentives, such as encouraging members to pin up their own notices in a participation section—a 'Swaps Corner', or 'My News' area, for example.

You could occasionally run a competition exclusively through the noticeboard. A small prize might be awarded to the first person to spot the spoof announcement, or the notice with the name of a football team in it. The noticeboard can be used as a 'signing up post', where people add their names to lists for this and that. Anything that encourages active participation will also encourage active reading of other material.

It can be helpful to number each notice and to keep a record of them, if there is any danger of their being removed 'unofficially' before their time. It is also a good idea to write on each notice the date it is placed, and the date it should come down, to ensure good circulation of information. If a notice needs to stay for some time, change its position from time to time. It will retain interest and attention, even if the content is familiar.

One person should be responsible for maintaining the noticeboard, or sections of it, to ensure that it is kept orderly and presentable. It may be sensible to make it a rule that only this person is allowed to add or remove notices (other than in the 'participation' part of the board), and that anyone wishing to add a notice should do so through the appointed person.

Photographic Material and Sound Recordings

Black and white, colour, instant photography, videos, cine films and audio tapes are all valuable resources for many aspects of publicity and public relations. As they can be useful on so many occasions it is a good idea to build up a supply of some of these throughout the year. You might appoint one person to be the Official Photographer, or somebody else to capture your various activities on video, or film. The results will be useful when compiling leaflets, annual reports, displays, presentations for Open Evenings . . . the opportunities are endless. The appointed person should have their costs reimbursed, for the materials can be expensive. He or she should be invited to all activities, events and occasions that might merit recording for posterity, and should be advised in advance of the circumstances of it (indoors/outdoors etc.) and of any particular shots you would like to have taken (such as the moment the Mayor inspects a particularly fine example of the group's work).

You should also discuss with your resident expert the sort of record you want. If photographs are to be taken for reproduction in newsletters, papers, etc., they should be in black and white. Colour photographs are best for displays, the archives, noticeboards and such like. Colour transparencies (possibly linked with a sound tape) or cine film are most suited to presentations such as Open Evenings where there is an audience of say 8 or more people. For smaller audiences than this, video is becoming a more convenient medium, as so many people now have access to video recorders. They are not suitable for larger groups, though, as the audience will have to crowd round the television set!

Although it can be expensive and somewhat complicated for the uninitiated, the value of building up records such as these cannot be stressed sufficiently. Plain words on the page can be very dull. A picture can make people **want** to read the words, and will often also communicate as much as many, many words. If you can find one or two keen members who would like to use their skills in these areas for the benefit of your group, encourage them all you can.

Newsletters and Magazines

These documents offer excellent opportunities to communicate both inside and outside the organisation. We are covering the subject in this section for convenience.

A newsletter or magazine (we will use the former term to cover them both from now on) requires a number of different skills if it is to be produced effectively. We will approach what is quite a wide subject through the eyes of each of the 'people' who might be involved. Clearly, it is unlikely that you will be able to field this number of people to run the newsletter, so some of the jobs will need to be combined. However, this method of approach should make it clear what is involved.

The Editor

A good editor will not be 'The Boss', but the leader of the team. His* role is very much that of co-ordinator, ensuring that everybody else plays their part, and that they understand how that part contributes to the success of the whole enterprise. The Editor has to decide on content. Some of the more useful and common features will include: An Editorial; Letters to the Editor; Dates for Your Diary; news about individual members; perhaps some form of competition (with or without prizes); some newsletters make space for jokes or cartoons to lighten the tone. All these will be intermingled with the main news, reports, articles and features.

The Editor will usually have to work hard to bully contributions out of people, but this is much better (for the reader) than if the Editor sits down and writes it all himself. Having said that, the Editor must live up to his name, and edit all contributions. He must ensure that they make sense, have correct grammar and spelling, and that they are factually correct. He may have to make them shorter so that they fit the space. This must be done with a combination of ruthlessness and sensitivity.

*The masculine gender is used throughout for ease of reading, and for no other reason.

The Designer

The designer, in discussion with the Editor, will arrive at the page size, shape and style for the newsletter. He will consider such matters as weight of paper, use of colour, design of the front page (especially the mast head with the publication's name), and the mix of text to photos or illustrations. He will brief the layout artist on the detailed appearance of each issue.

The Layout Artist

This person's responsibility is to produce the artwork from which the newsletter is printed. The text may be typewritten or typeset; it will need to be stuck down on the artwork, and headings will have to be prepared, perhaps with transfer lettering such as Letraset. Desktop publishing is gradually becoming more widely available, which is a way of preparing artwork from a computer.

Illustrator

It is very useful to have an artist who can produce line drawings or cartoons to fill spaces for which there are no words or photographs, quite apart from providing general illustrations to serve a particular purpose. Sometimes the illustrator will be given a free hand to pick out one section from the text; at other times the Editor will ask for a specific point to be made in the illustration.

The Typist

This is a vital role, whether you plan to print from typewritten copy, or whether a printer will be using the typewritten copy to prepare the typeset form. In either case, accuracy and clarity is crucial. However, no matter how good the typist, at least one other person should proof read the copy before it is finally passed for printing. Some of the most obvious mistakes seem to be the hardest to spot.

Contributors

There will probably be a few regular contributors who can be relied upon for their offerings. Others may be asked to write occasionally, perhaps about a specific subject. All contributors would be given a clear brief by the Editor as to what the piece should be about, how long it should be, the sort of readership it should appeal to, and any particular points that should be made, or examined. The quality of presentation and content will vary considerably, and the Editor must be prepared to wield the Blue Pencil, no matter who the author is!

Photographer

Frequently asked by the Editor (if he is on the ball!) to cover specific events and activities, the photographer will supply the newsletter with clear, black and white pictures to illustrate particular stories. Where possible these should be close up to the main subject, with plenty of contrast between light and dark areas, and not too much grey; they will reproduce much better then.

Printer

The printer will probably be your local copy shop, or general printer. He can be a valuable friend. Not only can he be sometimes be persuaded to do a job for a voluntary organisation a little more cheaply than usual (especially if it is a regular order such as a monthly newsletter), he will also be able to advise you on many of the tricks of the trade, to ensure that you reproduce the most attractive possible publication for the lowest possible price.

Distributor

It is so easy to forget that, once you have produced a newsletter, it has to be distributed to the readers. You should ensure that it is delivered quickly, on time, to everybody who should get it. If you are handing out copies at regular meetings, have some method for ensuring that if somebody misses a meeting they do not miss out on their newsletter.

You should also consider other people to whom your newsletter could usefully be sent. These might include local papers, the council, local businesses and other people who support you financially or in other ways. other organisations with similar objectives—anybody who might be interested in reading about your organisation, and who might benefit from it.

Accountant

All this activity costs money, of course, and somebody must ensure that expenditure is kept within the budget, that bills are paid, and that income is received. Income, if you consider it appropriate, can be obtained from selling the newsletter (a lump sum subscription for six months or a year is more manageable), and/or from selling advertising space.

Advertising salesman

If you plan to cover some of the costs of producing your newsletter through advertising it will be helpful to give one person the responsibility of selling the space. The spaces should be costed out realistically, striking a balance between the income you require, and what you can reasonably expect local businesses to pay, bearing in mind their other advertising in local papers. It would be unusual to be able to obtain a great deal of advertising, but two or three regular advertisers could make all the difference to your balance of payments.

Archives

Every voluntary organisation should keep archives—records of past events, activities, personalities. These should take the form of examples of all items of printed material, photographs, drawings, and perhaps small souvenirs and trophies. All these will have value as items of interest, and as a link back to the past. From time to time they may also be a source of inspiration, or even artwork, for new publications or promotions.

Summary

Develop mechanisms to ensure that all members are kept fully informed of past, present and future activities and plans.

These methods might include:

- Giving out verbal notices
- Fiery Cross
- Members' reporting back
- Newsletters and magazines
- Telephone contact
- Photographic and other archives
- Handouts and notes
- Noticeboards

External Public Relations

The purpose of external public relations is to encourage your target publics to be aware of your organisation, and to feel good about it. Public relations activity is often free, or uses money you were going to spend anyway. It is harder to control or measure in its effect, but it can often be better value than, for example, bought advertising space.

Good public relations does not just happen. Specific steps should be taken to build and maintain a good relationship with the public; these steps should be backed up with a constant flow of information (publicity) about your organisation's activities. This chapter is concerned with those steps, the next with publicity messages.

We have explored the fact that effective public relations has to begin from within the organisation, and that its members have to have good cause to feel proud of the body to which they belong. What active steps can we take to communicate this positive feeling to the outside world?

First, we should once again be clear about who precisely we wish to communicate with, and why. It is not realistic to expect that we can literally communicate with the whole world, nor is there any compelling reason why we should. With a little thought we can identify distinct groups of people whose view about our organisation matter. Here are a few; you may be able to think of others: potential members or helpers living in the community; people who may be called upon to support your organisation financially; the owners of your meeting place; the neighbours of your meeting place; members of the local Council; the umbrella body of your organisation. If you are ever involved in campaigning there may be other specific groups you would wish to target.

Once again, we should look back to the adjectives we selected to describe our organisation. Not only do we want our members to think of their organisation in these terms - we want the publics we have identified to do so as well. How can we take steps to get some or all of these messages across?

The messages will fall into distinct groups. Some will be concerned with the activities or the organisation, others with what it stands for, and what its members believe in. They will relate to what you do with the money you raise, how public-spirited you are, or how political you are. When you have decided what you wish to communicate you can start to decide the best way of doing so. There will be a number of possible methods, some better suited to some messages than others.

At the back of your mind you should always be aware that public relations is, as its name implies, about building relationships. The rules that apply to building successful personal relationships also apply when trying to build a relationship between an organisation and its publics. First appearances count for a lot. As individuals, the way we dress, speak and act says something about us as individuals. At the next level, our personality affects how people feel about us - whether we are egocentric or considerate, outspoken or reserved. Finally, people will come to understand our deeper beliefs and attitudes as they get to know us better. They will build a view as to the spiritual, cultural and political standpoints that we have.

All of these elements, which affect whether other individuals do or do not wish to associate more closely with us, will also affect whether our publics do or do not wish to associate more closely with our organisation. In an earlier chapter we discussed how the appearance of our meeting place, vehicles, literature etc., can affect the amount of respect and loyalty that members feel for the organisation They will also have a profound effect on members of the public, and their attitude

Uniformed organisations should be particularly aware of the public eye. If for any reason full uniform is not to be worn, then there should be some attempt to be consistent about the variation from uniform. All members might wear coats, for example, or all members might be allowed a variety of trouser colours. This might apply in cases of financial hardship, when the weather requires something more practical than uniform, or if the planned activity is not suitable for carrying out in full uniform. Many organisations go some way to solving this by producing T shirts or sweatshirts for their members to wear when uniform is not practical. This can look very smart, and need not be an expensive alternative.

The same principles should be applied to marching. If the members are turning out for an occasion where marching is an option (a Church Parade, for example), it should be made quite clear that everybody will strive to keep in step, **or** that nobody should behave as if they were marching.

Having laid the foundation for a relationship with the public by ensuring that appearances are acceptable, you can go for the next stage, which is to make sure that appearances are frequent. Personal relationships are more likely to grow if the individuals see each other frequently, and have opportunities to find out more about each other. The same applies to your organisation. Do not be insular, but seize every opportunity to participate in community activities. Enter a float in a carnival, a stall in the village fete, a team in the local sports or quiz contest. Arrange open days. Take your activities to the public and stage a demonstration of them in the town square, or library, or local park. Be seen. Be seen doing the things you usually do. Be seen doing them well.

Sometimes an individual member of your group will have an opportunity to participate locally - by representing the school in a contest, or being Mayor, or rescuing the Vicar's cat. Make sure that the matter is reported in the local press, and that the individual's connection with your group is also reported.

There will be times when these opportunities do not present themselves. However, it is likely that your organisation is still carrying out newsworthy activities, and it is in your interests to keep the local press (and possible radio) well informed of them. Press Releases before and after worthwhile activities, invitations to send reporters or photographers to particularly significant occasions, or photos and brief reports to the papers after an event are all ways of trying to ensure some coverage. You will not always be lucky, of course, but the exercise will not cost you much, and you will occasionally get some coverage which will make the members feel good, and which will also contribute further to the public image of your organisation.

Another opportunity is presented by reports which do appear, but which may not relate directly to your organisation. If a report, or letter, or photograph makes a point on which your organisation could have a view, there is a good chance to send in a Letter To The Editor, for publication. You certainly should do this if there is some adverse or incorrect information published about you, but there may be other matters on which you can comment. For example, a letter complaining about wanton damage caused by young vandals could be countered the following week by a letter from a Scout Leader pointing out the valuable community work carried out by the youngsters in his Troop. A report on the problems of loneliness in old age could prompt a letter from any one of a number of clubs for older folk, drawing attention to the services they offer.

Finally, but perhaps of greatest importance of all, are the individual personal relationships which your members have with other people. Each member should therefore be encouraged to communicate positively, enthusiastically and accurately about the organisation. If you need a new leader, or the loan of a minibus, you are more likely to be successful by 'putting the word about' through your members' contacts, than by placing a hopeful ad in the local paper.

Sometimes, of course, your members will not know the right people. A sensible approach over the longer term would be to identify specific key people that you would like to communicate directly with. These might be the local celebrity, or the Member of Parliament, or the person who owns a nearby large field which you would like to be able to use occasionally. You might identify a journalist, or a van hire company director, or a printer, whose friendship would be valuable to your organisation. As a first step, ask questions of your own friends to see if you know somebody who knows the target individual, and get an introduction. If not, see if you can take steps to get to know that person yourself. Invite them to functions, or try (sensitively) to have a word with them at another public function.

Summary

Build a positive relationship between the organisation and its publics.

Make sure first appearances count in your favour.

Make sure your organisation is frequently seen in action, and noticed by your publics.

Make the best use of the personal relationships of the members to forge links with the public.

External Publicity

Whereas External Public Relations was concerned with the development of a general relationship with the public, and encouraging them to have a good attitude towards your organisation, external publicity is concerned with the communication of specific facts. There are a wide range of methods to choose from when planning a publicity campaign, which are developed over the following pages. It is likely that you will benefit from using a number of them for any one campaign, as not everybody reads the same newspaper, looks at the same poster display site, or listens to the same radio station. If an individual receives the same message from you via two or three sources this is valuable, not a waste. It has been estimated that each of us is exposed to over 800 advertising messages each day. It is hardly surprising, therefore, that it is only the most striking and the most frequently repeated, which we remember. Against this background of competing messages, and in the likely situation that you do not have a massive advertising budget, your messages must be good, targeted and distinctive.

External Publicity

Most organisations produce some sort of leaflet to publicise their services or activities, or to attract new members, or funding, or support. As with all forms of communication the first requirement is to be clear about the document's purpose, and its intended audience. Both these factors will have an effect on how you state your message, and how you present it visually.

Leaflets and brochures

The content should be written from the point of view of the intended audience. Think about what you want to say . . then don't write it. Instead, rethink it from the point of view of the person reading it, so that you give added importance to what they will want to read. In this way you make it more likely that they **will** read it!

The nature of the document - paper size and quality, use of extra colour - will also depend on what the likely audience will expect. Some people may be offended by being offered a cheap and tatty leaflet; others may feel you are unnecessarily extravagant if you use thick glossy paper, and lots of colour. A happy medium can often be obtained by paying **slightly** more for a better paper, and using one extra colour cleverly, so that it has a lot of impact.

Any document should be 'user friendly' - the reader should be encouraged to read it by its very appearance. One of the best ways to achieve this is to use lots of white space! Even if the document becomes larger than you may have originally intended, the fact that there is less text on the page than there might have been somehow will attract the eye. Spacing between paragraphs and columns helps, as does a wide margin all round.

The use of headlines, illustrations and photographs is also an aid to reading. They give a clue as to what is coming, or they further illuminate what is being said. They add interest to the page and, again, reassure the eye that there is less reading to do.

Purpose of Document

When considering the size, format, style, content and presentation of the document, the costs of your plans should be weighed against its purpose. Clearly, something which will be used for some time, or which is to be distributed to influential people, or is an investment to provide further income or support, is worth spending more on than a one-off handbill. The important thing is to obtain the best possible product for the most appropriate price.

There are a number of leaflets, brochures, etc., which most voluntary organisations should consider producing. Some of the following suggestions may be appropriate to you. Some of them may be combined with others.

It is important that there is a leaflet which sets out the aims, objectives, activities and principles of the organisation. Specific information for new or potential members can usefully be compiled into a leaflet. An invaluable document is one which sets out the various ways in which people can support the organisation, both in terms of financial support which you would welcome, and any practical support and assistance you need.

Every organisation should produce an Annual Report. The Annual Report is seen as a chore which has to be done, and consequently looks boring and predictable. It is, however, potentially the prime 'sales document' for your organisation, setting out in words and pictures the types of activity you have been involved in over the past year, records of successes and achievements, thanks to friends and supporters, and details of the organisation's financial situation. All this can be presented in a dynamic way which inspires existing members, friends and supporters to go on to an even better year next year, and inspires **potential** members, friends and supporters to get involved in your thriving enterprise.

Once produced, your leaflets, brochures and Annual Report, etc., should be used. Make a list of all the people, and types of people, who should receive them. Once these people have their copies, think about other specific groups of people who might usefully have copies, or who might be interested in seeing copies.

Finally, consider other opportunities for placing the documents where a more general audience might possibly be interested. This first group might include members, supporters, the Press and Head Office (if you are part of a larger organisation). The second group could include people living near your meeting place, members of other local organisations with similar interests, or possible recruiting grounds like schools, or churches. The last group could include waiting rooms of all sorts, the library, and so on. If you have thought through all these possibilities before producing the documents, you will have a clearer idea of the number of copies to order.

Posters

Many of the previous points will also apply to posters, but there are some additional considerations. The key point to be considered is the intended location for them. Free space is limited, and in great demand. Possible sites will include shop windows, public places such as libraries and swimming pools, establishments such as schools and churches, and sometimes even the front windows of private houses. It will be seen that posters therefore need to be the right size to fit the space. If possible, it can be useful to produce two or three sizes, such as A4, A2 and A1. This will give greater flexibility when trying to place them. The largest practical poster should always be selected.

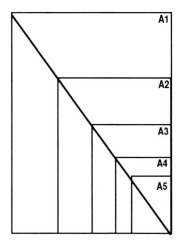

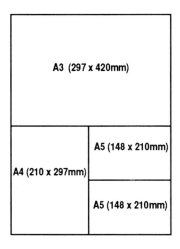

A poster should have as few words on it as possible, and something pictorial to attract attention. People will be passing by, and will only stop to look at your poster if they see something which interests or intrigues them. The wording therefore needs to be selected with great care, to make sure that it gets across all the key points, without presenting such a mass of text as to be off-putting. The headline should grab the attention immediately. Once again, therefore, it should be interesting to the reader, not necessarily to you.

Colour should be used if at all possible. If the posters are being screen printed this will not present a problem. It may be too expensive to use an extra colour if you are having a fairly small quantity photocopied or printed offset litho. However, it is quite practical to do some simple hand colouring afterwards, with paint or felt pen; the results can be quite stunning.

Handbills

These are most usually produced to publicise an event, and will often be smaller versions of the posters we have just discussed. Apart from being a good form of reinforcement, this can also represent a saving, by only requiring one piece of artwork for the two products.

There are many ways of distributing handbills, few of them entirely satisfactory. However, they do have a use for getting the message across to some people. They can be handed out in the street (but be sure to have people picking up those that get tossed aside - the litter will be very **bad** public relations!).

They can be delivered door-to-door by your members, or you can pay for them to be inserted into the local paper and delivered that way. They can be left in public places with permission (such as the library). Someone should check the supply from time to time to see if more are needed.

Bought Advertising Space

Newspapers, broadsheets, magazines, programmes, directories .... there is no end to the opportunities to advertise. Before you leap in, consider the following points.

Once again, ask yourself what the key message is, and who it is aimed at? The answer will immediately help focus your mind on the best location(s) for the advertisement. What kinds of people read the various papers, and what characteristics do they have that match your target audience - location, age, sex, interests etc?

Cost is a very important factor as advertising can be very expensive. For the given sum of money, how many people will you reach (what is the circulation of the paper)? Is a classified advertisement sufficient for your purposes? Can it be made more prominent by putting it in a box? Or do you need to go to an 1/8th page, or 1/2 page, or even a whole page advertisement? Look at other advertisements for similar things, and see how effective they are at that size. Will you place ads several weeks running for extra impact? If so, you may qualify for a series discount. It can be helpful, for example, to give a couple of weeks' advance warning for an event, followed by a final urgent re-minder. You may also qualify for a discount by simply being a registered charity. Ask for one anyway. If you are a charity, you need not be charged VAT on the display advertisement. Point this out when booking the space, as the person taking the booking may not be aware of the fact.

Consider the best position for the advertisement. If it is a coming event it is probably best placed in that part of the paper, as this is where people look when thinking of something to do. If the paper is carrying some relevant editorial, try to have your advertisement placed nearby. Note that sometimes an extra charge may be made if a special position is requested. However, it can be worth it.

As with posters, it is important that your advertisement contains something to catch the eye - a headline, border, or illustration. Once again you are competing with a large number of other messages. What is going to make yours stand out and draw the attention of the people who you want to attract?

Advertisements in papers and similar publications can either be set by the printer, or can be taken from artwork you supply. Small advertisements, classifieds, etc., are usually set by the printer.

If you are taking an 1/8th page or more it is probably worth having artwork prepared, to ensure that it is just as striking as you intended, and that the right words are in large, bold type.

Other Uses of the Local Press

Editorial is far more valuable than advertising because it is free, and because more people read more of it. You should therefore take every opportunity to obtain coverage in the press. Try to interest the editor, or a reporter, in preparing an interview about one of your members, or a feature about the work of your organisation. He will need a 'peg' to hang it on - an element of real news, but if the background story is interesting enough the paper will sometimes give it more space. Many papers have a "What's On" slot, in which they mention coming events, free. If your paper operates this, or a similar system, take advantage of it.

Other opportunities will be created by the despatch of Press Releases with really interesting and newsworthy information about your organisation.

You should analyse your local paper, and try to feed them what they want. Remember that the paper potentially **wants** to hear from you - it needs news. Try to make contact with the Editor of the appropriate section of the paper for your particular piece of news. Is it Business News, Diary, What's On, Local Organisation, or what? If one Editor or reporter is more likely to be interested in the majority of your stories than other people, try to discuss with that person the sorts of stories you may be able to offer, and how they should be presented. This is much more effective than a cold approach.

Remember that there are 'Silly Seasons' when the media finds it hard to get stories, and when it might therefore be more likely to use yours. This particularly applies around July/August, and immediately after Christmas and the New Year celebrations.

gry for news, local radio is positively
nean that you are guaranteed air time,
it does mean that there are many opportunities for you to use.
Check the list of programmes, and find out about each of them.
Phone-ins are a regular feature; perhaps you can call in and
make a point relevant to your organisation. You may even be able
to persuade the radio station to hold a phone-in (or some other
form of programme) on a subject of specific relevance to your
organisation. Many programmes also have "What's On" slots,
which you can make use of.

Publicity Seeking Activities

Sometimes it is possible to make news, both for people to witness
instantly, and for the press and radio (and perhaps even TV) to
report on later.

Press Conferences

A Press Conference is a standard activity of this nature, but you
must make sure that you have something really worthwhile to
say. The press should be forewarned with a press release stating
the time, location and subject matter of the conference, who will
be there, and what opportunities there will be for taking photographs. It should be addressed to the appropriate journalist by
name, or at least by title, and should be accompanied by a
personal invitation, and a map. The Release should say just
enough to whet the appetite and get the journalists there, but not
so much that they do not need to attend! At the conference, every
journalist should be given a Press Pack, containing all the
relevant information, and a contact name and phone number for
further information. Copies of the Pack should also be sent to key
journalists who did not attend. Members of your own team
should have name badges, as should any other key people
present. Those attending should be encouraged to sign some
form of record of attendance for checking up on afterwards.

Issue a Report or Survey

The issuing of a Report or Survey can be the reason for a press conference, or it can be issued directly to the press without one. A properly researched and balanced report on a subject of local interest and/or controversy will usually be mentioned by the press. The report should be clearly and attractively presented, indicating the name and appropriate qualification of the author(s), and detailing the basis for any figures, particularly statistics. A report can often be used to make a specific point, or to draw attention to a specific issue. It need not be the vital step to getting something done, but it might be a brick in the publicity foundation of a larger campaign.

A Seminar

Similarly, a seminar can be held to discuss a particular issue or topic. The most eminent and well known speakers possible should be invited, as should the press. The seminar should be well staged in an appropriate venue, with a good chairman, and either an invited or general audience. If possible, a verbatim report of the proceedings should be issued, or at least a detailed summary of the various contributions, particularly key points made, and recommendations or decisions arising.

Demonstration and Petition

Sometimes, a demonstration and/or petition can be used to indicate strength of feeling on an issue, and this will also give rise to publicity, both for the issue, and for the organisation behind it. A demonstration should be strictly organised and carried out with advice by police. Petitions should be carefully controlled so that there is clearly no abuse of them, such as the addition of spurious names. Again, presentation is as important as quantity.

Stunts and Events

These can be used to draw attention to a major activity, or to an issue, or to something your organisation is involved in. They can take many forms. Perhaps members will hand out leaflets about a theatrical performance whilst wearing their costumes. A demonstration of pioneering skills might be carried out by Scouts in the town square (by arrangement with the council) to draw attention to one type of activity they get involved with. The more unusual the stunt, the more attention it will attract. If the stunt has a strong visual impact it may result in pictures in the press (if you warn them in advance) and, as we have already stated, a picture is worth a thousand words.

Parents' Evenings, Open Evenings, Annual General Meetings

There are many occasions during the year when you can generate good publicity and public relations - or when you can bore a number of innocent victims stiff! As such occasions have a reputation for boring people stiff, you will need some very good advance publicity to ensure that you get a good turn out. Target the people that you most want to come, or the people most likely to come, (which is probably a completely different group!) and design the meeting and its publicity for their benefit. What location would they find most attractive, convenient or comfortable? What refreshments would appropriately be served? What special feature could be included to attract people to attend? Once these elements have been properly taken into account and publicised thoroughly, you will have done all you can to secure a good attendance . . . except . . . personal invitation cannot be bettered. If people receive a 'personal' invitation card they will feel that they **personally** are expected, and will be welcomed. If you or a colleague personally invite them, the likelihood of their attendance is greatly enhanced.

Having secured their attendance, let us look in a little more detail at what they are coming to.

Location of meeting

The location and its internal arrangement are important. Consideration should be given to the numbers expected, whether there are facilities for disabled people, toilets, catering facilities, and provision for any audio-visual equipment you may wish to use. Is the room small enough for speakers to be heard clearly, or is there a loud speaker system which works effectively? Arrange chairs in a slight arc; it looks a little more friendly than straight ranks. The speakers' table should be attractive, uncluttered, but with glasses and water, and a lectern if preferred. It is an idea to have a table at the entrance to the hall, so that people attending the meeting can sign in, collect name labels, or pick up literature. There may also be some form of display, although this is generally best situated at the back of the hall to avoid causing a distraction during the meeting.

The purpose, and therefore the content of the meeting will vary, but all should have an agenda. The chairman and all the speakers should be well versed in their roles, and each should know the amount of time allotted to their part. The chairman should be aware of all the times allotted so that, at his or her discretion, proceedings can be speeded up or slowed down to keep more or less to schedule. An agenda will include some or all of the following items: Welcome; apologies for absence; minutes of last meeting (taken as read if at all possible!); financial report; reports from various officers; questions; any other business; date of next meeting; votes of thanks (for catering, etc.).

When planning the content of the meeting you should be very clear of your objective, and try to ensure that every speaker contributes to the achievement of that objective. This might be to demonstrate what a thriving, lively organisation this is. It might be to get across a desperate message of underfunding.

The chairman will need to be particularly aware of the objective, and to stress this in his summing up at the end. Throughout the meeting he or she will chair carefully, allowing some free discussion and questioning, but no rambling or 'soap box' speeches. A firm but fair chairman is a great asset to any meeting.

It is helpful to have as much variety as possible in the presentation. Have a number of different people delivering reports or speeches, even if they could all be given by one person. Make use of such aids as overhead projectors, slides, flip charts, or actual objects to illustrate the points you want to make.

If there are some important issues that you want to get across, particularly if they are somewhat complex, make sure that all those attending the meeting leave with a pack of information - perhaps transcripts of some of the 'keynote' speeches, or information on the organisation and a letter setting out the issues with which the meeting was concerned. If the objective was to get people to **do** something , make quite sure that it is clear what they have to do, and make it as easy as possible for them

Public Speaking

Public speaking is an important skill, whether you are holding a meeting of your own, or addressing some other function. The following points may be of assistance.

The best advice ever given to a speaker was 'Stand up: speak up: shut up.' Be bold. When you are on your feet you are in charge, and the audience will listen. Do not be afraid to use notes - many of the very best speakers do so. It can be difficult to read convincingly from verbatim notes, however, and many people prefer to use keynotes - brief phrases to remind them of each next stage of the speech. A useful way of handling these is to have one, or at the most two, written onto each of a series of index cards. These are unobtrusive enough not to be a distraction to the audience, can be moved one behind the other as you speak so you need never lose your place, and will not rattle like paper if you are nervous!

Make sure you are audible - and that means not too loud as well as not too soft. If there is some form of amplification, seek an opportunity to try it out before the meeting or, failing this, see how other speakers use it and observe the results. They vary so much; in some cases it is best to speak very close to the microphone to avoid words being lost; in others this can lead to a booming sound that is unintelligible. If there is no amplification, address the back of the hall, even if nobody is sitting there. Thus your head will be held high, your speech will carry, and you will be (and seem to be) in command of the situation.

When planning your speech, be aware of the time you are allowed for it. If no time limit is offered ask for one. If it is still not forthcoming ask yourself how long **you** would be prepared to sit and listen to yourself. Twenty minutes is usually a maximum. Arrange your speech to suit the time available, and try it out in private to check the length. You will read silently faster than you will read aloud. You will speak more quickly on the occasion, when the adrenalin is flowing, than you will when rehearsing in private. When you have said all you have to say, finish on a high note to leave the audience feeling good, and sit down. If appropriate, allow time for questions. If you are asked one you cannot answer, do not worry, and do not bluff - it is too dangerous! A speaker will be more respected in the long run if he admits his own limitations, than if he waffles on about something he patently does not comprehend!

Displays

A good impression of your organisation, and specific activities and events, can be given by static displays placed in libraries, building society windows, churches, and other establishments where people might see them and where permission might be forthcoming. The display should be as professionally presented as possible, with plenty of visual information, bold headings, and small quantities of text. They are rather like an enormous poster in this respect. If possible they should be accompanied by a supply of leaflets and, better still, a person to answer questions, hand out leaflets, and generally create a bit of interest in the display. Displays can be bought, or hired, or made yourself.

Summary

Be clear about the purpose of your intended publicity effort, and the target audience.

Balance the cost with the purpose.

Make use of a number of publicity devices. These might include:

- **Leaflets, brochures, Annual Reports**
- **Posters, Handbills**
- **Press Advertising**
- **Editorial coverage in the press, and on local radio**
- **Publicity-seeking activities**
- **Meetings, public speaking**
- **Displays**

Copywriting

The ability to write good copy is an essential attribute for anybody involved in public relations and publicity. In this chapter we attempt to give some pointers to enable you to get your message across effectively.

The most important thing to keep in mind at all times is the audience. Who are they, and what are they interested in? Whatever you are writing, you must consider their needs, not yours. If you do this your piece is more likely to be read. If it is not read there is no point writing it anyway.

Next, you should be absolutely clear about what you want to say, and what are the key elements of the message. It is helpful to start with a series of headings, however long or short the piece is expected to be, and to put these in a logical order. As a rule, beginnings and endings are read much more than middles, so you should start **and** finish with your essential messages.

It is helpful to write naturally, and to avoid stilted or pompous phrases that you would never use in conversation, so that the reader feels you are communicating personally. At the same time, it is important not to use jargon or abbreviations that you and your colleagues would use regularly, but which will be meaningless, or at least confusing, to outsiders.

The same thing applies to long words where short ones would do instead. This is not 'condescending', or 'writing down to the lowest level'. However well educated we are, we all appreciate the facility of uncomplicated verbiage whilst assimilating information typographically presented (if you see what I mean!).

The length of the piece is almost as important as the way you write it. We will shortly examine different forms of copy which you might prepare; for each of them the rule is the same. Don't pad it out, and don't be so brief that you miss out important facts. You will frequently have flexibility in the amount of material you need to write. It is often best to write what is necessary, as naturally as possible, and then see if it fits the space available, or that it 'feels right' if space is not limited, as with a letter. If it needs cutting, you can select the less important sections, or find shorter forms of words. If it seems to need expanding, see if this can be avoided by using bigger photographs, or even white space. If you have to include extra material, try to find something extra to say, rather than rewriting your first version in a more long-winded way!

When you have finished your piece, re-read it, if possible a day or so later, when you come back to it fresh. Now, can long sentences be shortened, or bulky paragraphs be broken up? Can jargon or less familiar words that have slipped in be eliminated? Are spelling and grammar correct? Is the piece interesting for the likely readership, or is it just interesting to you? Is there something to grab their attention in the title, the first two lines, or the sub headings? Are all the essential facts there? By the time they have finished reading, will the readers still have a grasp of the essential messages? If possible, ask somebody else to read the piece, preferably somebody not as involved in the subject as you are, and ask them to consider it from the point of view of these questions. It is notoriously difficult to criticise and proof read your own work.

The next chapter is concerned with design, but we will say a word or two here about the presentation of the text, because it is important.

Typescript is greatly preferable to handwriting, even for all but the most personal of letters. It is easier to read; it lends more authority to the words.

Items for submission for publication (including Letters to the Editor, articles, drafts for your own publications etc.) should be typed, double spaced, on one side only of A4 paper, leaving a margin of at least one inch all round. There should be as few corrections and alterations as possible.

Items for Newspapers and Magazines

If you are preparing a letter or article for publication in a newspaper or magazine, you should see what sort of material they publish. How long are the average letters or articles? A Letter to the Editor should not include such phrases as 'I hope you will publish this because . . . ' This can be contained in the covering letter if you wish.

Articles and letters to the Editor are submitted in the hope that they will be published more or less in full. This is sometimes a forlorn hope, especially in the case of the former. You cannot expect that the piece will be published at all, nor can you be sure of when, nor will you have any real control over which bits are cut out (although there is no harm in indicating which bits you would least mind being cut if this were necessary).

Posters, Tickets, and other Shorter Items

When preparing brief pieces of copy such as posters, leaflets, tickets and invitations, make sure that you include all the essential information. It is all too common to see or receive such a document which omits the name of the organisation, the nature of the event, the address, date, time, or price. If you require replies remember to state RSVP. If you require a particular style of dress, remember to say so. Do not assume that people will understand your brilliant and eye-catching title; you may need to add a subtitle to explain it. "Organised Chaos" sounds a lot of fun, but for whom? "The Parent/Teacher Association Christmas Party" clarifies the matter, without detracting from the impact of the title.

Letters

Many people have a remarkable fear of letter writing, particularly 'formal' letters. The key is to remember that a real person will read the letter. Picture the person, decide what message to get across, then 'talk' to them, on paper, as naturally (and succinctly) as possible. It is not necessary to find a 'formal' form of words, or to try to emulate the stilted style of some of the official letters you have received. Far better to be yourself, and to communicate simply but effectively.

Forms

If you have to prepare any sort of form for other people to fill in, make it as user-friendly as possible. People fear filling in forms even more than they fear writing letters. The way the form is set out will ease that fear . . . or make it worse!

The following points should be made clear at the beginning:

1) That it **is** a form to be filled in.

2) Who should fill it in (anybody, or a parent, or only people attending a particular event).

3) Why they should fill it in (from their point of view).

4) To whom it should be returned when completed (and the address).

5) By when.

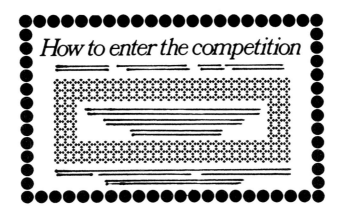

Questions to be answered should be numbered so that the reader is sure to complete all sections. Each question should be clear and unambiguous. If this is difficult in the confined space of the form, attach separate notes to explain certain questions more fully.

Spaces for answers should be the appropriate size for the answer required. This is a useful additional guide to the reader as to the amount of detail required.

Every device to simplify the task of filling in the form should be employed. These would include tick-boxes for YES/NO answers; 'delete which is not applicable' to save the reader having to write out long phrases, etc.

If the form is to be detached from a larger sheet or publication which contains information the reader should keep, make this clear. You should also ensure that important information is not on the back of the form, to be lost when it is sent off to you.

Copywriting is an art of communication. Style should vary to suit the occasion. Copy should be written with the reader and the reader's interests and needs in mind. It should be clear, unambiguous, and the right length for the purpose.

It should communicate.

Press Release

A Press Release is a different matter. A Press Release will ideally be on the headed paper of the organisation concerned; it will be dated, will state that it is a Press Release, and will have a title or headline which identifies the subject matter. It will be typed, double spaced on a single sheet of paper. It will have a contact name at the foot of it, with address, and daytime and evening phone numbers.

A Press Release should be as concise as possible. You are not endeavouring to write an article, you are endeavouring to excite a reporter's interest so that he writes one. The Release should therefore grab his attention, state the salient points enabling him to answer the questions "Who?" "What?" "When?" "Where?" "Why?" and "How?", and come to a swift conclusion. It may be helpful to include a short piece about the aims and objectives of your organisation if it is not that well known. It is common practice to include a statement or comment 'quoted' from an appropriate person. This adds life to the otherwise rather bald facts.

Photographs may be sent out with Press Releases. These should be good quality black and white pictures, ideally not less than 6 x 8 inches in size. Do not expect them back. Alternatively, you can include an invitation to the Press to send a photographer. You should also make your own arrangements to prepare photographs and copy in case the Press is unrepresented.

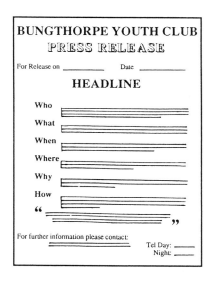

Summary

Always remember the intended audience

Be clear about what you want to say

Write naturally

Include all relevant information

Present it in an appropriate and clear format

Re-read; proof read; obtain an independent opinion.

Design and Production

A brilliant composition of words can be ruined or reinforced by the way it is presented on the page. In this chapter we are concerned with basic design considerations, and some hints on production techniques. Our objective will be to enable somebody with no formal training in design or production matters to think through the way a document should look, either with a view to actually doing the design, or to briefing the person who will be doing it.

What is design for? As far as the design of documents, posters etc., is concerned, its purpose is to attract the attention of a potential reader, and to present the material such that it is easy and comfortable to read. Sometimes design can go too far, and dominate the production, with the result that the viewer is far more struck by the design than the words, and misses the intended message altogether. You will be able to think of examples of this yourself - advertisements which have made a great impact on you, for example, even though you can't remember the product being promoted!

The design element therefore needs to be eye catching, but not dominant. What also should it be?

Cost effective. Some aspects of design and production which we shall go on to consider in more detail are very expensive. Sometimes it is justifiable to spend this money to achieve the effect being sought. Sometimes it will be out of all proportion to the purpose of the item being produced. For most printing processes, for example, adding one or more colours will considerably increase the cost. Non-standard paper sizes are more expensive to buy, and may present difficulties in printing. Cutting special shapes can be extremely expensive - even though it can be extremely effective as well. When planning your design, consider whether the likely cost is justifiable.

Step by Step Design

1)   Assemble all the information that is to be included in the production. It is important that this is fully comprehensive, taking in everything from the text to the address, the illustrations to the credits (such as authors' or illustrators' names). You will have arrived at some idea of the size of the production, which will relate to the way it is to be used, and to the financial restrictions upon you. A poster, for example, should be quite small if it is intended to be placed in shop windows, but much larger for big noticeboards etc. A leaflet to be handed out will benefit from being pocket-sized (or easily folded for the pocket) whereas a brochure to be left in libraries or waiting rooms, or which is intended to impress, should be altogether more substantial.

Having considered all the material to be included, you will have to decide if it will all fit, and how many pages will be needed. Remember that in most circumstances you will have to work in multiples of four pages, as each sheet of paper will be folded in half, and have two sides.

2)   Decide what information is to go where. The key factor is to decide what is most important, and where that element should therefore be placed. Try to ensure that all the elements follow logically, so that somebody coming to the document for the first time will know how they are supposed to use it. In a booklet with a number of pages, try to ensure that each page looks balanced beside its neighbour.

A helpful way to visualise a booklet is to prepare a 'flat plan' - a series of boxes which will help you to visualise which pages face each other, and which pages are printed back to back. An example is given for an eight page booklet - the same principle can be used for any number of pages.(*Fig 1 - overleaf*)

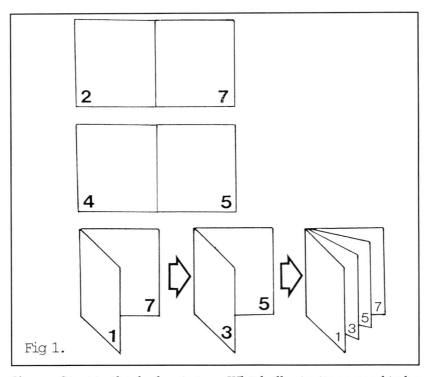

Fig 1.

3)   Start to think about sizes. Which illustrations need to be larger, either for impact or clarity. How big do headlines need to be in relation to sub headings and the main text? Will everything still fit?

4)   If you are using more than one colour, consider how this can best be used for impact and effect. It is tempting to splash colour about all over the place - in fact it is far more effective used sparingly.

5)   Before making final decisions, stand back and look at the whole production. Is there sufficient impact in the right places, so that the important facts stand out? Is it eye catching yet easy to read? Is it balanced, or is there too much emphasis to top or bottom, left or right? Finally, to return to the point at which we began, is all the information included, or has anything vital been missed out along the way?

Let us now consider some of the elements of design in a little more detail.

Text

There are three ways in which text can be altered - through layout, size, and typeface.

Layout is simply the way the text is presented on the page. What choices are open to you? The margins can be justified or unjustified (if the left hand margin is justified the first letters of each line form a straight margin). Justifying the right hand margin as well gives the text a more formal - and perhaps less lively - look. The text can be broken up into blocks - by leaving lines between paragraphs for example. It can be helpful to set the text out in two or more columns rather than straight across the page, in the same way as a newspaper. Combining these formats can be effective.

The size of text can be crucial. To an extent, the amount that has to be said will influence the size of type used to say it. However, small text can be very difficult to read. Surprisingly, large text can also present problems. Our eyes seem to be attuned to reading text within certain size ranges, and outside those ranges we get confused. Type sizes are measured in 'points'. The diagram illustrates some examples of different type sizes.

'Typeface' refers to the shape of the letter. There are many fancy typefaces available, but for the main text it is generally best to use a fairly standard, uncomplicated design. The principle choice is between 'serif' and 'sans-serif'. A serif is a little 'flourish' at the beginning or end of each letter. A 'sans-serif' face does not have this little addition, and tends to look a little simpler and perhaps less old-fashioned. The diagram shows some examples of different typefaces to choose from.

SANS
SERIF

Avant Garde Gothic Medium Condensed

Avant Garde Gothic Medium

Avant Garde Gothic Bold Condensed

Avant Garde Gothic Bold

Bookman Bold

Bookman Bold Italic

Bookman Bold Condensed

Caslon Black

Century Schoolbook

Helvetica Medium Extended

Loose New Roman

PROFIL

Rockwell 371

Souvenir Medium Italic

Times Bold

144pt 38.0mm

72pt 19.6mm

60pt 16.1mm

El

48pt 12.8mm

Ea1

36pt 9.5mm

Ea1

24pt 6.4mm

Ea1

14pt 3.4mm

Illustrations

'A picture is worth a thousand words', it is said. Certainly, pictures will add considerably to the force of your production. Before you decide to carry pictures of various sorts, consider the points raised later in this chapter on production techniques, as there may be limitations on what you can do.

Photographs need to be good, clear, black and white pictures with plenty of contrast in them. These will print well. A poorly defined photograph with lots of grey areas will simply look a bit of a mess on the page.

Line drawings and cartoons need to be well executed - few people have the real ability to convey an image with simple strokes of the pen. It may be that an 'amateurish' line drawing will devalue your production.

Diagrams and charts can sometimes convey information which would be very confusing if presented as ordinary text. If using this method of illustrating your point, make sure that the reader knows which bit of text refers to which diagram.

You should consider whether each illustration needs a caption. Some will be self-explanatory, others will need to be put into context. You may wish to indicate that they refer to a specific section of text, unless they are for general effect, to add an additional dimension to the printed work. Borders can be a useful form of illustration, dividing sections of text, or drawing attention to specific elements. Again, avoid overdoing it, or the effect will be lost.

Headings and Sub Headings

It can greatly assist the reader to have specific sections of the text picked out with headings., These indicate that a new section is beginning, and roughly what it is about. Alternatively, the heading may be somewhat enigmatic, so the reader **wants** to know what it is about. Newspapers are prime examples of the use of this technique. Look at them objectively to learn a few of the principles. Headings should be picked out from the main text by being bigger, or bolder, or underlined, or centred . . . whatever suits the layout best.

Colour

There can be no doubt that colour, judiciously used, adds greatly to almost any publication. First, remember that for most printing techniques there is no need to print in black at all - the whole thing could be printed in one attractive colour. Similarly, the effect of colour can be given by printing in black, but onto a coloured paper. This will not cost significantly more, and yet it can lift the appearance of the publication substantially. When considering either of these options, beware of one important consideration. The text must be easy to read. It is no accident that most printing is in black ink on white paper - the contrast makes it easier to read than almost any other combination. If you do plan to deviate from this, you should still try to use a dark colour ink, and a light colour paper.

If you plan to print primarily in black, and add one or more colours, this will add to your costs, but also to the effect. You may use the colour on the illustrations, borders, headlines - wherever you think it will have the best effect.

Paper

The choice of paper and card is quite enormous, and you should ask your printer to advise you on the quality and finish most appropriate for your planned usage, and budget. You should consider whether a light-weight paper will suffice, or a thicker paper might be necessary. This particularly applies if you plan to print on both sides - the paper should be thick enough to stop print showing through from the other side. Also remember that you can select a tinted paper if this seems appropriate - it is even a surprise to see how many varieties of white there are!

Costing

There are a number of factors to be considered when costing the production of a piece of printed material, and you should discuss each of these with your printer. You would be well advised to obtain two or three quotes from different printers to ensure that you get the best deal, in which case it is vital to ensure that they are quoting for exactly the same job - that is, each is aware of all the elements of it.

The costing should take account of origination charges - the cost of preparing the artwork used by the printer. You may do this yourself, or you may ask the printer to do some of it - such as having the text typeset. If you are using two colours you will need to produce an overlay - a separate sheet containing only those elements to be printed in the second colour. The price will need to include the cost of making plates used in the printing process, and the cost of the printing itself. You may wish to have the production folded, stapled, perforated or cut, and each of these operations will incur additional charges. There may be a delivery charge if you cannot collect the finished work, and VAT will almost certainly be quoted separately. Ask the printer about this quite specifically; also ask him whether VAT should be charged at all, as some printing work does not attract this tax.

Printing Techniques

It is helpful to have some idea of the printing techniques available to you. You should discuss your requirements with a printer or two so that they can advise on the most appropriate technique for your job, and the advantages and limitations of that technique. Few printers will offer all methods - you should find out which your printer specialises in.

One of the most basic forms of printing which is becoming less common (although it is still the mainstay of many voluntary organisations) is duplicating. A stencil is cut on a typewriter, then transferred to a duplicator for printing. It is possible to add headings and borders by hand, but this is less than satisfactory. There are machines which will make stencils by photographic transfer, but they are expensive and not commonly found. The result is adequate, but only just.

Far more common now is the photocopier. Almost every High Street has an instant copy shop offering photocopying facilities. Photocopying enables you to reproduce anything you care to place on a piece of paper. Even photographs will come out, although they will not be quite as good as those in newspapers. Photocopying is quick, quite cheap (particularly for small quantities) and very versatile. It is often all that is necessary for basic printing jobs.

For better quality reproduction, longer runs or the use of colour, offset litho is generally the best choice. Plates are made photographically from your originals to a very high quality, and they are then used to transfer ink to the paper on the press.

Letterpress is a technique whereby pieces of metal type (or metal blocks for illustrations) are used for printing. On a small scale this technique is mainly used for such tasks as invitations, business cards and similar small-run projects. Having metal blocks of illustrations made specially is quite expensive.

Screen printing is used generally for larger items such as posters. This is a comparatively inexpensive way of using two or more colours on a job, although it is only suitable for fairly short runs. Text and line illustrations can be reproduced, but not photographs.

For small numbers, you may care to consider some hand finishing yourself. For no additional cost other than your time you can enhance a production with the careful use of felt tip pens, highlighter pens, or even paint and brush. If you are even more ambitious you might stick on little bows, or glitter, or paper stars . . . the possibilities are endless.

Summary

The purpose of design is to attract attention to the words, and not to detract from them.

Ensure that the cost of the proposed design is justified.